1999

C

happy birthday, dear bert...
relish this little
book of
uncommon
love and
uncanny wisdom...
you have (our) (my) love,
Melissa
and
Mindy

Also by Stephen Gaskin

Monday Night Class (1970)
The Caravan (1972)
The Grass Case (1974)
Hey Beatnik (1974)
Sunday Morning Services, Vol. 1 (1975)
This Season's People (1976)
Mind at Play (1980)
Amazing Dope Tales (1980)
Rendered Infamous (1981)
Haight-Ashbury Flashbacks (1990)

Cannabis Spirituality

including
13 Guidelines for Sanity and Safety
by
Stephen Gaskin

HIGH TIMES BOOKS
NEW YORK

Portions of this book have appeared in somewhat different form in *This Season's People, Mind At Play, The Grass Case* and *Sunday Morning Services on The Farm, Volume One.*
Editor: Steven Hager
Art Director: Frank Max
Managing Editor: Chris Eudaley
Copyeditor: Steve Wishnia
Proofreaders: Dean Latimer, Gabe Kirchheimer
Cover Painting by Alex Grey
Stephen Gaskin photo by
Andre Grossmann/HIGH TIMES Archives

Library of Congress Cataloging Publication Data
Gaskin, Stephen
Cannabis Spirituality
1. Religion, U.S. 2. Marijuana/Cannabis/Hemp, Spiritual uses in the U.S. 3. Hippie Culture, 1966-1996

ISBN #0-9647858-6-2

FIRST EDITION 1996

SECOND EDITION 1997

DEDICATION

I dedicate this book to Jerry Garcia. He was a friend of mine and I will miss him. I wish he had been wiser about his dope and stayed with us longer.

While my two biggest boys and I were on our forty-day and forty-night car trip to the Arctic Circle, they questioned me about many things. They wanted to know why I didn't have any money, what with all the things I have done. They wanted to know all about who-all I have been married to. They wanted to know what I believed.

They wanted to know why I have a strong tendency to cry at the Jimi Hendrix Star-Spangled Banner. One of the understandings we came to was where it was about the Grateful Dead.

They finally caught on when they said, "It's not even just the music, is it?"

I said, "That's right! Even though I consider Garcia to have been one of the virtuosos of our time, it wasn't just the music."

It was showing how to be a huge, successful, big deal in the real world on hippy terms without selling out. It was doing the revolution with a sense of humor and a wall of sound and no guns. It was deliberately spreading love at thousands of watts. Ich bin ein Deadhead.

THIS TRUE LOVE IS REAL AND SHALL NOT FADE AWAY.

R.I.P.

CONTENTS

1
ENLIGHTENMENT IS ORDINARY REALITY

God is the universe. We are all parts of the whole. When we act with our own natural intelligence, God is acting. When we have a new idea, we are the part of God that thought that new idea.

The universe itself is God's mind, and the flow of everything is God's thoughts. And praying means being an intelligent synapse in God's mind, a synapse that won't trigger for violence or injustice.

Religion is a *generic* term for how we relate to our universe and how God and our universe relate to us. There shouldn't be anything deeper than your religion. Your religion is how you really get along with folks—not what you may claim your religion is.

Your religion ought to make a difference to you in your daily life; it ought to make it easier for you, not in the sense that you don't have to try, but in that it *makes sense for you*. If you're not getting along with your kid, it ought to help you out with your kid. It ought to help you out during childbirth; it ought to help you out with the death of somebody who's close to you. It ought to help you through the heavy passages of life.

Religion is something that lives in the hearts of the people. Our country needs a massive religious revival. This may seem strange to say when we seem to be covered up in fundamentalists. That, to me, is evidence that our spiritual technology has fallen into disuse and rust from so many years of neglect. We're so ignorant about religion that many people are just pretty much suckers for anything that comes by, because they need religion so badly.

Our culture is overrun with superstition. Any time I hear some person who was late for the plane that crashed say, "I guess God had more work for me to do," it makes me want to say, "And what about all those people who made the flight and crashed? Were they all bad people? Were they all supposed to die?"

The idea that God is some old white-haired Englishman who hides behind one-way glass and zaps an occasional human who bugs him is pernicious superstition.

That kind of thinking also leaves the door open for religious warfare. It leaves the way open for people to think there could be a God who loves Christians better than Buddhists, or Jews better than Moslems, or Catholics better than Protestants and takes sides in human wars. It is a cause of *jihad* or "holy" war.

In Islam they talk about the will of Allah. I say that the only way to really know the will of Allah is in retrospect.

You can listen to television preachers for hours, and never have even a smell of real religion or enlightenment. They are, as the welldrillers sometimes say, "a dry hole."

We must, in a proper practice of religion, recognize the incredible dedication of try-ing to pass enlightenment hand-to-hand for thousands of years. We have lines of apos-tolic succession that have come down to us twenty-five hundred years in the Buddhist, two thousand years in the Christian, twelve, fifteen thousand years in the Vedanta. One of the basic Christian beliefs is that when you become a Christian, you are plugging into an energy source that has a two-thousand-year-long extension cord plugged back into what was a guaranteed clean energy source. This is worthy of respect. There is also clean and holy energy that is right here in modern times. It is also worthy of respect.

There are spiritual levels of experience that people are heir to and in times when there's a lot of material success in the world, folks sometimes forget to tune into these fine things and lose the knack, maybe for generations at a time. Whenever it comes back, it's always a big flash.

If you touch that spiritual vibration, it will touch you back. There isn't supposed to be an intermediary between you and God.

A lot of folks don't remember or realize it, but the Methodists came to this country because they were in trouble in England. The reason they were in trouble was because they just didn't pray and ask for forgiveness, but they had methods which they used to elevate themselves spiritually or get high, basically. In this sense a Methodist could be translated as a Yogaist. Yoga is the difference between where you are and where you want to be. It can mean standing up straighter for some and not standing up so straight for others. Some of the silliest stuff in the hippy movement is the result of people trying on each other's prescriptions.

People would like for karma to be about justice but it's really not. Sometimes the karma gets very obscure—as when a baby is shot in a drive-by shooting. The karma in that situation is the parents were so poor, or black or Hispanic, that they had to live there. We cannot turn our back on that kind of karma and say it's just one person, one karma and it's all okay. We have to say it takes the deployment of considerable intelligence to make that kind of karma be just, if you can at all.

I honor the old religions, like Buddhism and Christianity and Judaism and Islam, because they're enshrinements of a heavy thing that happened in the hearts of a certain generation. I like to study these faiths through their saints. The mystical sect of Christianity is called the Gnostics.

Buddhism has Zen. Hinduism has the Yogis. Judaism has the Hasidim. The Moslems have the Sufi. If you study their writings, you will discover that they talk again and again and again about exactly the same phenomena, the same experiences, the same realizations. They've obviously been to the same territory.

I always think that Buddhism is like a trick or a riddle. If you fall for the Buddha, you missed it. The Boddhisattva is where it's at. Supposedly, the point of Buddhism is liberation from the wheel of rebirth and leaving the strife of the world for nirvana. The Boddhisattva is one who could leave the wheel of existence but elects not to and stays and works in the world to help others reach liberation. Maybe it's just the American hippy in me, but the path of the Boddhisattva seems the more noble. To me this is the real inner meaning of the Vow of the Boddhisattva:

The deluding passions are inexhaustible, I vow to extinguish them all.

The way of the Buddha is unattainable, I vow to attain it.

Sentient beings are numberless,
I vow to save them all.

The truth is impossible to expound,
I vow to expound it.

By the time I get this far, I generally lump them together as,

"I vow to shovel shit against the tide forever."

I think that goes along with the Zen idea that if you're in the right place it doesn't matter whether you have clairvoyance, or whether you have clairaudience, or whether you can see auras. All that stuff is completely optional. I also believe the ordinary man can think an enlightened thought and be enlightened in that instant and enlightened men can think ordinary thoughts and not be enlightened every instant.

It isn't that I was into Yoga or meditation so much. It's that I was ransacking religions looking for goodies. I went through what I thought was the secret stash of each one. That seemed to me to mostly be in the neighborhood of meditation and enlightenment.

I am a believer in free will. I am not a

believer in predestination. A belief in prophecy of the future robs us of our free will. When you insist on believing everything will always come out right, you give up your freedom to affect the outcome.

I love the ethical teachings of almost all the religions, and I love the psychedelic testimony of their saints. But I do not believe in any of their dogmas.

I think each one of us has a non-shirkable obligation to figure out the world on our own as best we can. The way we behave as a result of that investigation is our real and practiced religion.

Jesus and Buddha were both really populists. Christ reformed the religion of his time by throwing the moneychangers out of the temple. He was for the common people. A lot of people don't realize that Buddha was exactly the same. He was the son of a king and joined the common people. The religion of that time had been cooking for 10,000 years, and they had huge temples and powerful priests and were top-heavy with priest craft. It had become a class-ridden religion. Buddha taught an equality-based religion. Like Jesus, Buddha made no distinction between a beggar or a king.

Among all peoples everywhere and throughout time, there is a normal bell curve of distribution of intelligence and talents. The scientists say it took about as many people down through history to build up to how many people are here now.

According to this concept, there should be among the five billion people who are alive right now those who are as talented and as smart and as together as anyone you can name from past history. Among the present population of the planet there are equals of all the saints, all the martyrs, all the teachers, all the gurus, all the avatars. We have all those talents among us in the present crew. Which means, if you're trying to fight the good fight and be responsible with your vibes, then you can be a living Zen Boddhisattva right now. There is good holy energy common to our time frame, not just to past ones.

It's not complicated or unusual or weird to know what God wants. God wants justice and freedom and health and happiness and equality for everyone. If you know that's what God really wants, you'll help out along those lines.

Religion starts heart to heart, mind to mind, eye to eye, between real people. Some people talk about fancy trips where they went to fancy places, but the fanciest places I've seen were in somebody else's eyes. You can look in somebody else's eyes and find truth right there. Truth doesn't have a brand name on it; it's like water— runs in every creek and falls from the sky.

And religion is like water too. The way you can check it out is the same way as water. If it freezes at 32° and if it boils at 212° (at sea level), and quenches your thirst, then it's water. If religion is compassionate and if it excludes nobody and if it doesn't cost money and if it really helps you out in the here and now, then it's real religion.

I don't believe in too much religious para-phernalia. I think that the most important thing to understand about the life-force energies is that you can move them with your mind—you don't need a tarot deck or a Ouija board to connect. I don't think it's necessary to make what you call "a leap of faith." The evidence is manifest right now. And even if you're still self-indulgent in ways, you know it's there. Everybody knows it.

Some people think it helps if everyone has some form of spiritual ideation or sense of universal family and relates to each other as spiritual beings in human form. That seems a little faulty and high Brahmin to me. The human form *is* a spiritual form and is noble and worthy of respect.

We here are all obviously the same kind of creatures. Consciousness works like a holographic image. If you take a small corner of a hologram, you don't see a small corner of the picture, you see the whole picture. The resolution is not as good as the whole hologram would be, but everyone is seeing the same picture. It's not like some people are seeing it and some people aren't. Any other way of looking at it seems to point to an intellectual spiritual elite, which I cannot abide. Goodness is not an intellectual question and is not confined to a spiritual elite. Even if the resolution varies, everyone is still seeing the same picture.

I don't think a spiritual initiation is something you pay for. And I don't mess with palmistry or astrology or the *I Ching* or any oracles or divinations, because complicated systems of magic have nothing to do with the spiritual plane other than to help you remember it's there. That plane exists independently, and if you're of good will, you can inhabit the spiritual plane.

There's a religion that is perfect and true and has no errors in it, and all man-made religions are unsuccessful attempts to copy that religion. It exists unwritten in the hearts of the people for all these millions of years. You can tell the people who know about that religion, because it works for them in the here and now, and they look sane and healthy. You can find people who practice that religion any place, and you can tell who they are, because they look well manifested and they're friendly and they're sane and they're functional and they're able to actually do things.

Don't think of enlightenment as struggling along this road for years and years and then there's a big golden gate and you go in and ancient elders hang a big jeweled doohickey around your neck and say, "Zap, you're enlightened!"

Some people teach that enlightenment is something other than reality. There's a set of teachings in *Tibetan Yoga and Secret Doctrines,* by W. Y. Evans-Wentz, about the things that are the same. For instance, it's the same whether you have psychic powers or not, the same whether you can read the future or not. Enlightenment is ordinary reality, which does not mean that it's not rare and precious.

A lot of people are so involved in themselves, in their passions, their griefs, their sorrows, their desires, that they never see what is really there. Looking in the advertisements in the spiritual magazines, you see one for a guy who says that you haven't had true enlightenment unless you have had the vision of the little blue seed pearl. If you come to him and take his course, he'll teach you how to have that vision. There's another guy who says you have to hear the inner sound. There are a bunch of other people who have similar criteria that they say must be met in order for there to be enlightenment and it can only be met through them. This is just setting up "brand names" to distinguish their path from other paths.

Psychic powers and enlightenment haven't got anything to do with each other.

In fact, following psychic powers can lead to craziness. In the Sixties, a lot of us, including me, got silly at various times. The way I am now is I run more down-home and tolerant and I trim away at the superstition whenever I can.

Watching television can put you into contact with much of the sorrow that goes on in the world. These are scary times. Some people teach that enlightenment means you look away from reality instead of into it. That's not right. You look into it, and you help as much as you can. When you get tired and ground down until you can't put out good vibes, take a rest from looking at it until you feel restored, and then go back to work.

When I was living in San Francisco, I went to a hospital to see a friend after he'd had a motorcycle wreck. Well, actually it was more than a motorcycle wreck. He had taken the bike without permission and had a wreck with a stolen Cadillac and the bike and the car had burned in the intersection. He got out with a broken leg. When I went in, I had this feeling I shouldn't disturb all the poor victims. Then a nurse came up, took a look at how sorrowful I seemed and teased me into improving my vibes until I realized that the hospital is like the real world, too, and that even if you are broken up or ill, you still have to come on to the world with a good heart and not drag it down. One of the ways to tell if there is any enlightenment is whether there is any service or not. There is so much heartache and suffering in the world that it is important not to add to it.

The first prerequisite for enlightenment is a real heavy sincere desire that will make you go through whatever changes are necessary. Usually these changes are a lot simpler than you think they're going to be. This desire explains why millions of hippies stood on their heads, or shaved their hair, or did 150,000 prostrations, or any of the various excesses and extremes that we did in the Sixties, thinking there was some formula we could follow to become enlightened. Mostly paying attention to other people instead of one's own self is a great help.

I never met anyone who took enlightenment seriously until I got around hippies. I was around church people, but many of them lie constantly. They talk about miracles that happened in some other time and place. Once in a while a preacher can move a congregation and get them stoned, but most of the established churches are dry holes. No energy happening there. Most churches don't teach anything about enlightenment. They want you to sign a contract and give them money like an insurance company. The most dangerous thing about religion is self-righteousness. After all, what was the Inquisition but an orgy of self-righteousness, torturing people to death to save their immortal souls?

Enlightenment comes and goes. One of my favorite Zen statements is:

I do not seek after enlightenment;
neither do I linger where no
enlightenment persists.

It's not like climbing a mountain and once you've done it once, you're the person who's climbed Mt. Everest. Sometimes on a good day you know where it's at, and you've got a nice serenity on, and you stone people with your presence. Sometimes you don't.

Enlightenment means you aren't easily driven to rage, you don't let people push your buttons and you don't use emotion as a tool to manipulate other people. It means you are not in the game for money or fame but for love and justice.

Another thing about enlightenment: You can't have a teacher at one end of a room and a bunch of people at the other end, and the teacher is enlightened and the people are not. It doesn't work that way. The psychic vibration naturally goes into a group resultant of all the energy fields on contact. These fields flow like water into their natural shape. If most of the people are sane and good, and they talk good stuff, they're all enlightened. If anybody in that room tastes enlightenment, they all taste it together. In that sense enlightenment is more like daily bread. It sustains you as you go along. Enlightenment is like fire and water. Wherever in the universe you find fire or water, they follow their own laws. And if you see a little piece of fire on the end of a matchstick, and a huge building burning, it's the same thing.

One of the most important communities on Haight Street, that illustrated spirit in a very real way, was one that I have never heard anyone mention in all the years since then. It wasn't a rock band or a dance troupe or a political commune.

Just a block or two from Haight was a group home for people who had certain mental disabilities. I say "certain" because whoever had put this community together had done such an excellent mix of people that I always thought they must be very good at their job.

There were about eight or nine in the group. There were a few with Down's syndrome, a couple of microcephalics, one or two who didn't show anything physically who were probably technically morons. I suppose you could say "retarded" but that wouldn't quite do justice to the gestalt they created. In their aggregate, they were better than that. They coped, together, better than any one of them could have done alone.

They would go for walks on Haight Street in a tight little group. They would stop at each corner and confer about what to do, twittering like a flock of birds. They would watch the traffic light intently and when it turned green they would run across as if they didn't quite trust it not to change and catch them in the street.

Sometimes one of them would lag behind to stare or wonder at the scene on the sidewalk, which was, after all, San Francisco, Haight-Ashbury, 1968: Neo-cowboy hippies; bell-bottomed, paisley-draped flower children; shaven-headed, yellow-robed, gringo monks; bikers; drag queens; grass dealers; and speed freaks.

When one of them noticed he was behind, he would run to catch up to the collective strength of the group. They stood out among the high-drag hippies of the time. They wore crew cuts, clean white t-shirts, new blue jeans and clean white tennis shoes. They were crisp and, even, cute. They valued their sanity and competence because it was not taken for granted but was something that they worked together to achieve.

Generations of hippies saw these people, who became known as the "Hobbits" after the characters from the Tolkien trilogy. They became a walking, talking, living metaphor for community. They were, in effect, a Mahamudra, or great symbol. The first time I ever saw the Hobbits, they were pointed out to me by a young hippy girl who understood them perfectly. She said, "Look how they take care of each other. What if everyone took care of each other like that?"

In retrospect I think the Hobbits may have been some of the most significant teachers in the whole Haight-Ashbury scene. In the Jewish tradition, the *tzaddik* is an enlightened being. It was said that God would never destroy the world as long as there were at least 36 of these just men and women. Some of these *tzaddikim* lived in the open as famous teachers or musicians or rabbis. Others never revealed themselves and were called "hidden." The Hobbits were a commune of hidden *tzaddikim.*

Each day in their walk down the street, they would be seen and remarked on by scores of hippies. They probably made more difference in the vibes on Haight Street than formal teachers who came from India to share the hippies' juice.

They were selfless and they were good trippers. They didn't come down in 12 hours like most hippies did. Coping was a lifetime trip, and they did it with grace and good vibes. Who could say they did not taste enlightenment?

One thing about calling enlightenment "ordinary reality" is that it might lead you to believe that it's universal. It's not. That's why if you read about it in an old book, it might have several chapters about how whoever would pass on this knowledge to even one person would acquire more merit than all the grains of sand of the Ganges, stars in the Milky Way or leaves on all the oak trees in Tennessee.

2 CREATING THE GENTLE RITUAL

I live on a 1,760-acre farm in Summertown, Tennessee. The Farm is a community of over 300 people of many ages, races and backgrounds. We deliver our own babies and bury our own dead. We've found ways to support ourselves so that our work is more or less seamless with our life. What we do for a living doesn't conflict with our religious beliefs. This is called right vocation.

We began meeting together 30 years ago in San Francisco. We started off knowing little more than that there was something other than the material part of existence. When we first got together we were like a research instrument. We read everything we could on religion, magic, telepathy, superstition, psychology, extra-sensory perception, fairy tales, collective unconscious, folkways, math and physics.

We started putting this thing together, and then it started to get recognizable as the pieces fell in. We saw that it looked like every religion. We realized all of the best minds in history had been devoted to religion and all of the records that had been preserved the longest had been devoted to religion and everything that seemed to be the most central to all cultures was religious.

We began to call ourselves the Monday Night Class because we met on Monday nights. After four years the class had grown to 1,500 people. Then I was invited to speak at a number of colleges and churches around the country, and 200 of my friends decided to come with me. We left San Francisco on October 12, 1970.

We talked about what was the most important thing in the world we could talk about right then. We talked about God, we talked about politics, cannabis, love, sex and marriage, death and religion, nonviolence, telepathy, subconscious and enlightenment. The first speaking engagement was in Oregon, the next in Minneapolis, Michigan, Vermont, and all around the country.

Some places we'd talk about spirit and nonviolence, some places we'd talk about nonviolence and spirit, depending on what kind of place it was. By the time we got to Atlanta, Georgia, the media came out to our rest stop to talk to us.

They said, "We hear you are about peace. We are very afraid of biker wars and dope turf wars on Peachtree Street. Maybe you could come in and help pacify our scene."

We did our best. We came to Peachtree Street and I talked in four different halls, moving to bigger halls as we overloaded each venue, all afternoon and evening. I talked about bad dope and violence and keeping their scene clean. I pointed out the guys in the back of the hall selling pill dope and speed.

But something else was happening to us while we were doing all that, which was that we were living on the road in a caravan of sometimes as many as a hundred vehicles. We had better than 50 great buses, and we were this giant organism in the veins of the freeway system. Society couldn't figure out what kind of antibiotic to take to get rid of us. We went 12,000 miles like that.

We traveled for four months, and when we got back to San Francisco something had happened to us. We had metamor-

phosed. We weren't quite city folks anymore. There was no place to park the caravan. The second Sunday morning was a
drivers' meeting, and we were going to
stow and go. We were going to Tennessee to
find a farm, because we'd become a village
on the road.

Six months later we bought a farm in
Tennessee. We settled into the farm and
talked about how to treat all of our neighbors and how to get along with them. We
worked for them, we traded equipment
with them and made friends. We've been
trying to implement old-fashioned instructions like "love your neighbor." For some
neighbors, we found, loving them is to stay
out of their face and not to bother them.
Other neighbors we can love by being close
to them. We've been in planting, growing,
harvesting and building agreements with
our neighbors out to a several-mile radius.
An old farmer who lived about 20 miles
away lent us $10,000 so we could get a
Greyhound bus and go out and talk to
everyone, on tour with our Farm Band,
because he likes our influence on young
people. We're friends with our county and

state officials, too. The county's built a road for us two and a half miles into our farm, and we worked with the state health department (as well as the United Nations children's team) in developing a sound vegetarian diet. I am friends with T. C. Carroll, who was the sheriff when we came to Lewis County and who busted me in 1971 and who, later on, married me and Ina May in his office. I am friends with Sonny Jones, our local FBI agent. He is close enough to us that he understands us pretty well. He gave us a beautiful "rap sheet" that is so nice I could send it to my mother. I am friends with our new TBI (Tennessee Bureau of Investigation) agent who told me that his father was our *first* TBI agent. He said, "Dad told me you were all right."

Why the Farm is here, and why it's doing it like it is, is because we've been following a spiritual path. We've found through our collective experience that there are levels of experience that people are heir to, that people are supposed to be able to experience, and that these are spiritual things. What we found when we were studying religion was that people have certain spiritual needs that must be served, so religions are created to serve people. Somehow religion has to serve a human being's needs. It has to help in birth, in marriage, in death and in growing up.

When we first started learning about it, we didn't know what it was, but we've caught on to what it is now. At first we thought we were going to have to make a set of rules on how to handle it because it was so far out of the ordinary, but then we found there was a set of rules already. Our Bible is written in the minds of the people. All the ways that people be and all the things that happen to people, and the loves and births and deaths and angers and hatreds—all the things that can possibly happen to mankind—have happened time and time again over the last hundreds of thousands of years. All those things have been figured out so many times that we all do *too* know what to do, and it isn't so mysterious.

We learned that if you really want to change the world, you have to change your soul—you have to change things from the spiritual level. That's what Jesus meant when he said, "The prophets of old say unto you, 'Thou shalt not kill,' but I say unto you, thou shalt not be angry with thy brother." He had the vision that could perceive the telepathic plane where anger is just the same as violence. He was saying that you're responsible for your thoughts, just like Gautama Buddha when he said you're responsible for your body, speech and mind. All those teachings are really plain if you look at them from the point of view that they were trying to tell people that there is another plane of existence that's as important and as real as the material plane.

Our church has various precepts. We believe we're all one, and that the Holy Spirit is identical and one in all of us. We believe there can be no final or perfect enlightenment for anybody until there is for everybody. When you know that, you try to help everyone, equally and impartially. We recognize that mankind has a common spirit, and that everything that takes place is the agreement that takes place in that common spirit; that whatever harms any of us harms all of us; that we can't have folks we like and folks we don't like, and friends and enemies—we can't have that at all.

We are all one, and we can share one soul, and we can communicate telepathically and vibrationally, and you can know your brothers and sisters right straight across, one to one, wide open, no barriers, if you have enough nerve to look in their eyes and say to yourself, "I'm sorry if I was ever cheap or bad to you, and if you find it in your heart, forget it, forgive me, I want to be with you anyway." And just open up and let them come into your mind and soul.

We believe that how you be makes a difference in how it is for everybody. There is something you can do and it's within your power to do it; and if you do it, it makes a difference.

We believe that you can change. If you can change yourself, you can change the universe. The capacity to change yourself is the heaviest factor for world change that people have.

We believe that you don't need to be ruled by anger or fear. If someone comes on angry to us, we try not to come back angry to them, we go off and do the thing that we do to get cool: meditate, smoke cannabis, go for a walk in the woods, and get our peace back. That way we take anger out of the system, and no one has to suffer from it again. It's the same way with fear.

We don't believe you have to kill animals to be healthy. From one acre of ground raising cattle you can get 140 pounds of protein per season, and from one acre of ground growing soybeans you can get 1,400 pounds of protein per season. This is a ten-to-one advantage for everyone involved. If everyone were vegetarian, there would already be enough to go around and no one would be hungry.

We don't take welfare. We have to begin to take responsibility for the whole of mankind, and we can't do that if we can't even take responsibility for ourselves.

We believe that work is a holy meditation and the physical expression of love. We say that God supports us by keeping us high enough that it doesn't bum us to work.

We believe that giving birth is a sacrament. We do it all naturally with our midwives, and it's a sacrament that we return to the family.

They say that entropy is the running down of life, and that the universe is run-

ning down. We believe the universe isn't
going to run down, because life is going the
other way. Entropy and life force are a stable
pair that maintain the universe eternally.
Life force is what makes a baby live, it's
what makes you heal, it's the Holy Spirit.

I don't use tobacco or coffee or alcohol.
I don't take any speed drugs, like
Dexedrine, Benzedrine, Methedrine, or
Ritalin. And I don't use any of the barbitu-
rates, or heroin or cocaine or morphine, or
anything derived from any of those things.
We recognize that those things block you
off from what's happening out there, and
they're self-indulgent and addictive.

I don't take chemical psychedelics—
nothing from a laboratory, nothing anybody made. I use only the grown, organic
kind. They come from God that way. All
over the world, for thousands of years,
wherever psychedelics are grown, religions come along with them. Cannabis,
peyote and magic mushrooms are the
classic organic psychedelics. We believe
that if a vegetable and an animal want to
get together and can be heavier together
than either one of them alone, it shouldn't

be anybody else's business.

We believe in psychedelics and that they expand your mind, but all the rest of the stuff that beatniks take is mostly a social fad. Don't lose your head to a fad. The idea is that you want to get open so you can experience other folks, not close up and go on your own trip.

We think we're supposed to enjoy the universe. But we're supposed to enjoy it in such a way that it doesn't tear up the universe or us. It's disrespectful to God to enjoy the universe in a way that destroys the universe, or to enjoy the universe in a way that destroys yourself.

We have to deal with attachments. We are in this world of constant change and yet we get attached to people and things. Much of the trouble in this world is caused by people who don't know when to let go. I get attached too. I like to advocate the Band-Aid-on-the-hairy-leg treatment but sometimes it's hard to get up the nerve to do it. I think you have to be habitually frank with yourself so you know when you're being attached and you don't BS yourself into thinking you're doing something different when you are being attached. Then if you know what it is and you're honest with yourself about it, it's easier for you to recognize it and to say;

"Well, this is causing trouble and it's ignoble too, and I will regret it later, so why don't I quit now?"

The way we're living and what we're doing is trying out a philosophy to see if it works—trying out a religion and a way of life to see if it really functions. That's how you can tell if a religion works or not. Does it make it for you day by day? Is it something you can live by? Is it something that will be there when your kids are born, and is it something that will be there if you happen to lose one? Is it something for real? Does it have any juice in it?

For my part, I didn't know I was going to get religious until I was about 30 years old. I had a master's degree and had taught a couple of years in college. Then I started taking psychedelics. I took psychedelics because I wanted to have a religious experience. I had read a book by Aldous Huxley called *The Doors of Perception* that said you could have a spiritual experience that way. What got to me was that I realized that, of all the experiences that I had ever had in life, none of them had ever been what I would call a spiritual experience.

The first kind of thing I saw on psychedelics was all kinds of forms, shapes and colors happening. Then it got so I didn't see that kind of thing so much. I just started seeing what was really there in front of me, real good, better than I had ever seen it, so that I understood everything that was happening in it. I suddenly started feeling that the magic of psychedelics wasn't in some other world or some other place, but that they put you in communication with other people. Most of the really heavy things that happened to me were when I was stoned with other people—when it got all honest, when it got really high and all golden and beautiful and bright and white-colored under the power of truth; when you looked at them and saw true compassion, and you knew they really did love you, and you knew you really did love them.

There is a plane of existence which can be felt by a human being which is other than the three-dimensional material plane. There are many religions that tell us of people experiencing that plane. Those are the stories of miracles and visions and revelations, and there have been many religious teachings telling us how to get to that plane.

Being *stoned* itself, the very sensation of *stonedness*, can be sent as a telepathic message. That's what caught my attention. The *contact high* is when someone can feel the effects of a psychedelic just by coming into contact with someone using it. I checked it out and found it was there, it was real, to the point where I realized that it's not an unusual thing. It's what's supposed to happen to you in church when you have communion.

During my highest psychedelic experiences, I learned the key to life and death, heaven and hell. That's real—that's transubstantiation. The miracle of transubstantiation takes place with a psychedelic just like it is supposed to with the Host. And that miracle is so heavy and so real that we should approach it with the greatest veneration, the greatest awe and the greatest respect.

We don't say that psychedelics are a panacea or that they're necessarily going to get you enlightened. What you manifest has to do with your own personal moral structure—you can manifest on the side of the angels or you can not, whatever you choose, it's a matter of free will. So it takes character and integrity to get high on psychedelics. That's why we don't say they're *the* way. But we have to say that they're *a* way.

When we want to feel close to the Holy Spirit, we get together before the sunrise and take communion. We sit in meditation for an hour and smoke cannabis if we have it. Meditation is learning to be quiet and shut your head off long enough to hear what else is going on. And when you get quiet for long enough, you get so smart that you suddenly realize that you've never been that smart before in your life, and it's a better mind that you have access to.

As the sun crests over the hill, we chant the OM together. The OM is a hymn without any words—you take your simplest, openest, most honest note and let it out. You sing out in prayer. The OM is sort of like the people's anti-bad-vibe machine. They say if you took all the sound in the universe and listened to it all at once, it would sound like the OM.

It's like if an airplane passes overhead, an

old propeller type, and you listen to the hum of that plane and start humming in frequency. When your voice matches up with the plane, you tap into the airplane's power and feel your humming come on stronger and louder and more resonant. As those vibrations cross and hit their pitch place, it comes on really strong and powerful.

The OM is supposed to be spelled A-U-M, and each letter in it is supposed to be significant of one of the parts of the Hindu trinity, so when you're chanting the OM you're also invoking the trinity: Brahma, Shiva and Vishnu. With the deepest AAAAA you can vibrate the solar plexus. The UUUUU helps turn on your throat chakra, which is your universal love chakra. That's what getting all choked up is about. On the MMMMM part, you're supposed to put your front teeth together so it vibrates your cranium.

If you create an energy wave in the physical plane, then higher and finer vibrations can ride on that physical plane vibration, like a carrier wave. You can assist yourself in elevating your consciousness, getting stoned, by humming a note that opens your throat and vibrates your head. So as you do the OM, you make a physical vibration happen, from there all the way up through the higher chakras. And by the time any paranoia has filtered through, it's stoned, and you're projecting high, because it's just energy and all you do is clean it up, and then you can run on it.

The OM reduces the tension level in the people around you, helps make them to be less uptight, makes them easier to get along with. When you bring up the physical vibration, it brings up the electronic/spiritual/telepathic vibration. I love a large OM because it fills up all the harmonic niches. It's really a complete thing. And the OM in your mouth gets stronger as the other people's OM comes down your throat and vibrates with yours.

With cannabis, you can have one joint and two people, and you get higher than if one of you smokes it. It just works that way. And if you share it with six people, you'll still get higher than if just one person smokes it himself.

There's a real gentle ritual, in that it gets passed from hand to hand with the gesture of "I'm passing something precious, and we're sharing communion with it." You can look around and recognize yourself in every eye you look at.And you begin to realize that it's not some once-in-a-lifetime revelation you get to experience the One, but it's the daily bread—it's what makes it possible for us to make it on the planet, that we can look around and catch somebody's eye and know that we're all really in this together.

Sometimes I just take a joint and go out into the woods and sit down and smoke it. I see everything that's there, and just see where it comes from and see that it's absolutely meaningful. I go into communication with God and the universe.

Another reason I use cannabis is because I find open religious experience to be one step closer to God than open Bible, which was a step closer to God than having a Bible of Latin that only the priesthood understood.You can go to the experience and learn it for yourself. You can use cannabis as a sacrament—not as an end in itself, but as a holy tool to help you to experience reality. Cannabis opens you up and leaves you compassionate. People really need to get compassionate if we're going to make it on this planet.

3 CLEANING THE TERMINALS

In thinking about human electricity, I realize there is human electricity and there is human electronics. In the material plane, you have to make a distinction between electricity and electronics. Electricity is the movement of energy from here to there, and the changes you put electricity through—like making it more powerful, alternating current, direct current. Electronics is another field; it takes electricity and not only moves it around and makes it more or less powerful, it modifies it and flavors it. Electronics makes for flavors of electricity.

In that way, depending on what part of your electricity you are talking about, people can resemble a storage battery, a capacitor or a radio. The battery is a phenomenon of electricity. The original kind of battery was a box lined with metal and a plug that went into the box, insulated so the plug did not touch the box in any way. Then, attached to that plug without touching the box itself was another piece of metal. Then you fill the box with a liquid acid, which becomes the only connection between the outer metal box and the inner metal piece hanging from the plug. So an electro-chemical reaction takes place, and you can put one wire fastened to the pole on the box and the other wire fastened to the piece of metal that makes the pole in the plug, and you can touch those two wires together and get sparks. You get electricity right there.

A capacitor is almost as if you had a storage battery without the liquid. You can build an electrical potential up to a certain point, beyond which it would have to discharge. You can put juice in a battery over a period of time, and tap it out over a period; with a capacitor, you put juice in over a period of time, and you tap it out all at once, in one spark. People can do that, too.

But to contain a vibration, you don't have to be considered just as a battery or a capacitor. You can be considered as a radio, which is a standing wave of electricity. You create a wave, and you have it stand there. A stationary wave with a strong, definite shape. When you run electricity through that system, it creates a wave that stays the same. And you can modulate that wave, so it is the same as another wave somewhere else, and the waves will resonate together.

There is a difference between straight body electricity, transmitted by rubbing and touching, and electronic energy, which you do not have to touch because it transmits by radio.

In the Bible, Jesus was walking down the road and suddenly stopped and turned around and said, "Somebody touched me."

And the gathered disciples said, "What? What?"

He said, "Somebody around here touched me, got into my juice. Who is that?"

And a lady standing in the crowd said, "I saw you walking past and I felt that you had a lot of holy energy, and I needed to be healed, so I touched you as you went past."

He turned around to His disciples and said, "See? I told you somebody touched me."

He was a capacitor moving along

through the crowd, and she just tapped Him out. It was cool with Him. He just wanted to keep the books. If He knew where it went, it was okay.

Now, you're supposed to be self-generating. You're supposed to be self-charging batteries. You can't only exchange energy from battery to battery. One way we're supposed to be able to charge ourselves is by Tantric Yoga, or sexual magic. Actually, you don't really charge yourself; you just get pure enough and you are able to zap into bigger stuff and get charged from that. That's your thing.

It is generally supposed that the presence of gender or of the yin and the yang of things is common throughout the manifestation and you should seek to be aware of it when you are building anything. It has to do with what we think of as attitude, masculine or feminine. It has to do with the characteristics of building materials, rigid or flexible. Many modern materials are made of flexible and rigid materials together. Systems of martial arts explore the implications of the yang and the yin.

The biggest thing for us as ordinary

humans is to learn the understandings and feelings of opposite sexes. Our time is marked by terrible misunderstandings between men and women. It is a lifetime study. You don't get a Ph.D. for it, but if you're good at it you could get a good marriage and interesting close friends of both sexes. The secret is not for men to try to be yang and for women to try to be yin. You already are. The secret is to learn to respect and flow with the other pole.

The polarity of electricity is another manifestation of gender. It's almost the same in the material plane of electricity as in the spiritual electricity, because *we don't really know how much electricity there is*. The potential is infinite. The amount of electricity that we are sitting in right now is some millions or billions of volts. For instance, an electric generator has a core and a magnet, and it runs one of them around the other and it generates a potential of electricity. The earth is 8,000 miles in diameter and about 7,000 miles of that is iron. And the moon is another chunk of similar kind of stuff, and here they are spinning around each other like a giant generator, and that creates an electrical potential which we here call zero. So we are living in a field of unimaginable intensity, which we just happen to be used to, spiritually as well as electrically.

When someone comes to an experienced mechanic and says, "My battery is dead, and my car won't start," the mechanic doesn't immediately assume the battery is dead.

He says, "You check your terminals?"

The terminals connect the box and the piece in the middle. Those connections are called the positive and negative terminals. The mechanic knows it is in the nature of electricity—because it is so powerful and electro-chemical in action—to tend to corrode the terminals. So you have to clean the terminals now and then, so they don't get corroded. In fancy equipment, you try to make terminals of metals that don't corrode, like silver and gold.

When somebody comes to me and tells me, "My old man (or my old lady) doesn't get me off any more, I think the battery's dead," I ask them, "Check your terminals?"

Which is, in human terms, your relation-

ships. In most cases, we find not dead batteries, because if somebody really had a
dead battery they wouldn't start at all. But
love is so powerful and so heavy, and people are so incredibly complicated, made of
beast and angel, God and ape, that love,
strong by nature, can corrode the terminals
if you are not careful.

For instance, back at the Family Dog
rock'n'roll hall in San Francisco when they
were first trying to get it to be a rock hall,
Chet Helms was running around San
Francisco hustling as hard as he could, and
his friends were helping him hustle in order
to get this rock hall together.

He had one friend who owned an old
battered Cadillac limousine, so the dude
with the limousine got himself a funky
chauffeur's hat, and he started driving
Chester around to make all his appointments with all the people he was trying to
get together. So he would pull up in this
black Cadillac limousine, and the dude, his
friend with the chauffeur's hat on, would
pop out and go open the back door, and
Chester would step out in his Afghanistan
coat with white fur trim, carrying his snake

staff, and go magic up a few partners for this rock'n'roll bread. So he played this game with his friend—and in between appointments, they were turning on together, passing a joint from the front to the back seat of the Cadillac.

Then the hall started happening, getting it together, and Chester wasn't traveling too much; he was hanging out at the hall. But that guy liked the game, and kept wanting to do it. So he became the guard to the door to the performers' room. When you'd come into the room, he'd give you a great sweeping bow, with a "Come on in, sir," and like that. And everybody was in the spirit of the game, and it was fresh, and they'd put a whole bunch of energy back into it, and there'd be a lot of juice in it for the guy at the door and everyone else as well.

Well, that went on for a few months, and after a while, people got in a hurry to see Chester, and the guy at the door didn't quite put as much juice out as he used to, and it got to where he became a real one of what he was mocking. He just opened the door for a lot of people, who said, "Thanks," and went on through and did not put full value into it—and he almost fell out of love with the whole game. It lost the form and the juice it had before, and it came apart on him. He didn't really want to be obsequious to anyone and be a servant; it wasn't what he had started out to do at all. In the pressure of the situation they lost the spirit of the game, and he did become a sort of servant, and he didn't dig it.

Well, being a good hippy, he saw that he had to metamorphose. He became Captain of the Upper Deck and was indispensable, the one who knew the moves and ceremonies in making rock'n'roll happen. The game was afoot and fun once again.

Suppose you get married, and you've been married about a week and one of you pops out of bed before the other and fixes a good breakfast and spreads it out and comes on strong that they really love you, and you come on strong how nice it is to be taken care of this way, what a groove, and I love you too. Boy, you'd better take care of it, and don't let it get worn down and make it pedestrian and ordinary and let the juice run out of it until it becomes something like, "Toast, hold the coffee. Later, Baby."

So if the car doesn't start, check your terminals. You have to scratch down through all the corrosions until you get to the bare, raw metal. When you're cleaning the human terminals, you have to get through all the corrosions until you get down to the quick. Sometimes, the way you can tell when you get down to the quick is someone goes, "Ow."

And you say, "Oh, I got to the quick. Sorry about that."

Then you know you have to back up and back up, and give room and give room, and try to open up and have no pride. Pride is one of the worst corrosions that can happen to people. It's mostly copper sulfate and lead breaking down in batteries; in people, it's pride.

Mostly, when couples hassle for a long time, it's because they're prideful. One, or both, of them maintains their position and proves they were right.

"They did something to me, and I'm going to wait until they come through first. It was their fault and I'm going to wait until they apologize."

If I feel like I'm not straight with who I'm

in love with, my ammeter is just way down in discharge as long as that situation continues. I don't want to sit and wait for some event to happen before I try to get that back up into the charge zone again. I want to start doing what I can do right now. If that means I have to say I was wrong or dumb, or I'm sorry, or please forgive me, or I don't care, or I forgive you and it was okay, it wasn't heavy compared to what a heavy thing we're supposed to maintain between us.

You better do what it takes to not lose "your real good thing." Those good things can be hard to come by.

No pride, no pride, that's a place where nobody can afford a speck of pride.

4 TURNING ON

When I was 17 and in the Marine Corps, I went and visited my cousin, who lived in California. He had been smoking grass for a while, and he wanted to turn me on. It was a good impulse, in a way, but he got a little carried away with it.

We got in the car and went out on a lonely beach. We stood on the sidewalk by the sand and burned this joint together.

He wanted to be sure I got high. He had me take a long, strong toke and then squat down and blow on my thumb. After a few of those, he had me floating and really banged. Then he took me back to the car.

As we were walking back to the car, we came to the curb. I stopped at the curb for a moment and looked down at it.

"Look down over the edge," my cousin said. "Look at the rapids. See the white water breaking around the rocks—*waayyy* down there at the bottom of the canyon, where the rapids are."

While I was looking at that, as he was telling me to, he walked around behind me and pushed me off the curb.

I fell six inches, and landed stiff-kneed, jolting all my vertebrae. I was not at all ready to land in six inches.

He thought that was funny, and took me off in the car. As we drove off down the road I said, "Take it easy; it's my dad's car."

"Hee-hee-hee," he said. "I'm going to drive fast. I'm going to drive *fast*. Ah hah! You see how *fast* I'm driving? I'm going to drive *real fast!* I'm going to drive fast, and scare you! *I'm going to drive really fast!*" And it seemed to me that we were going *very* fast.

He jacked me up and got me very nervous and weird over that we were going to go fast. But while he was doing that, he never went over about 25 or 30 miles an hour.

Then we stopped and parked somewhere, just to hang out and trip together for a while. He said, "You know, I can just control you. I can make you high and I can bring you down. I can lift you up and I can bring you down."

He started telling me that, and I said, "Aw, come on, you can't either," and things like that.

He started telling a bunch of jokes and saying funny things, and he got me stoned and giggling and high. And all of a sudden he said something to me real gross and unkind. Just cut me off short and froze me up.

"See? I can bring you down. I can get you high."

While I was still sitting there trying to digest that, he got me to where I could laugh again. He got me back up. But I never trusted him again. I couldn't, after that; and I identified that with grass for a long time. (If he ever reads this, I hope we can burn one together as grownups and put that childish crap behind us.)

We got home—we were staying at his house. I went in, and I had the most incredible raid on the icebox that I have ever had in my entire life. I went into that icebox and had a chicken leg in one hand and was slurping up cold mashed potatoes with the other. I was eating peas that were stuck together with globs of congealed margarine. I ate for a long time, just indiscriminately eating everything on two shelves of that refrigerator, before I slowed down. I thought, *That was really fun.* That was the first real feed I'd ever been on—my first feast. The first time I ever enjoyed eating to that extent. It was just delightful. It was a real help to me, because I was a skinny non-eater. I consider that effect to be technically medicinal in my case.

But I was afraid, because of what he had done to me. He had violated the guide position.

I didn't understand that at the time. All I knew was that something wrong had been done to me, and that I was not going to do grass again.

Ten years later I really turned on. It was with a good dude who was one of my real early teachers. George was an artist and art history student. Not in college, necessarily, although he took some college courses. But he was an artist already, as well as a student of art. He had some *beautiful* old art books, and he showed me ancient art with folks with mushrooms floating over their heads. He showed me that in many cases, the auras of saints were designed to look like a mushroom, or to imply that the mushroom had something to do with that. He showed me all these ancient paintings of an obviously psychedelic religious feeling. He was really a student of religion, too. He looked French, had long hair before most folks did, and was cool.

He turned me on to my first successful grass. It was my birthday, and a bunch of my friends were giving me a party. It was real nice and friendly, and George came and brought a carved German meerschaum pipe, which had some kind of smiling face on it and a little lid. He loaded it up with Acapulco Gold, and said, "Just take a good hit of this."

"I ain't really done any of this," I said.

"You do this," he said.

He was such a nice guy, and I liked him so much, that I just did it, although I had been *fried* ten years previously when I had last tried it.

We got all stoned, and I knew he was too, and every time I'd look into his eye, I'd see that stonedness looking back out at me, and it would make us both laugh. I was very telepathic with him, just right there together. At some point I got so telepathic that I said,

"Man! I feel so telepathic with you! Do you feel like that?"

"Yes! Yes! It's where it's at, man! Ain't it

neat?"

There is a kind of tequila called *tequila almendrada* that's yellow and golden colored. It felt like I had a *tequila almendrada* yellow filter on—yellow and goldy everything.

I just cruised through that night. And in the morning, I felt good; there was no hangover, like I usually had from boozing, because I hadn't boozed. I'd forgotten to drink because I was so delighted to be stoned. I thought,

I'm probably not going to drink very much anymore.

And I'm probably going to do this a lot.

5 THE NATURAL CEREMONY

Cannabis can be the focus for a free-lance, ad hoc spiritual meeting. A group of people, partaking of the good herb together, not perhaps even thinking of anything spiritual, can find themselves coming together in communion. This is not a communion of words but a communion of minds and spirits and souls. It creates a simple down-home ceremony that they can relate to instead of dogma. With grass, if nothing else, you have agreed-upon phenomena, and an agreed-upon source for them. It's a natural plant. It comes from the natural universe.

I don't believe in imposing ceremonies on others. I think you should learn to recognize the natural ceremonies when they're happening. Sometimes they just come along, and here's one going on right now, and you find yourself behaving ceremonially. A real master of ceremonies is

someone who knows the natural ceremonies, knows when they're about to happen, when they should happen, and
facilitates them in the here and now.

When I understood that about myself, I
saw why I had such a heavy impulse to
jump into things, like an *espontaneo* jump-
ing into the bullring to whip off his suit coat
and cape the bull a few passes.

The best ceremonies are put together by
necessity. When life is heavy and the juice is
flowing, people are more careful how they
handle their minds and bodies. If you're out
in no-man's-land with a gun in your hand,
you spread out five yards apart. That's the
social shape for that kind of stress. And
there's other times where you sit in a circle
and hold hands. And those times can be just
as heavy.

A friend of mine, while enduring what
was called Agni Yoga, was caught in a very
powerful *mudra* or tableau. The table was
shaped like a "T." The "master," a gringo Yogi
we called "Superdoop," sat above the cross
of the T with the rest of the teaching staff to
his right and left. My friend sat at the foot of
the leg of the T. The "yoga" was essentially

criticism and ass-chewing. You can see how the body language of the seating amplified the effect. When my friend told me about it, I thought it was a psychic ambush, but effective.

Under stress, some people naturally sit down, lotus up and straighten their back. That's a person assuming a *mudra*, or meaningful gesture, as well as a good technical way to handle psychic energy. If you have a group and life gets heavy for them, they have to assume a group position to work from. The group assuming that *mudra* is performing a natural ceremony created on the spot. Sometimes we are shown a tableau like the wise men and baby Jesus or the Last Supper.

Many times I have been at a party at a middle-class house, and at a point late in the evening, when the serious party people are all that's left, someone breaks out the grass. Usually, during the evening, people sat on the chairs and couches and sipped their drinks and chatted. When the grass comes out, the people notice they are too far apart to pass the joint or pipe comfortably, and they slide down off the chairs and sit in a circle on the rug. It's also just to be more intimate. When a group of friends assume such a position, it is a communication that is pre-verbal. It says that we are loving and trusting friends together and we are going to share this experience. That's the real stuff.

Back 20 years ago, we thought this is going to be plan A: Everybody gets high, we become the Yellow Submarine and it's peaceful from there on.

Well, plan A was a nice concept, but we didn't exactly pull that one off. But plan B was, if you remember, that from among all these young hippies around here smoking all this dope, there are going to be people who will run for political office 20, 30 years from now. Some of these very people who are puffing this boo are going to be presidential candidates! And they actually are.

In 1996, the President, Vice-President and Speaker of the House have all turned on to grass. And even if Bill Clinton doesn't actually have the moral courage to try to legalize reefer, at least he and Al and Newt know in their hearts that we are not crazy or criminal. So, I feel pretty good about the idea that the struggle is not over and we can have the courage to keep on going.

I like to think of folks like us as spiritual revolutionaries. Being revolutionary about spirit means that you're not into lords and kings and hierarchies. Being spiritual about being revolutionary means that even though you are committed in a deep and serious struggle, you will be decent in your tactics, while doing your absolute best. So this struggle goes on and I know it's going to be a more than one-generation fight.

In San Bernardino many years ago, Pete Seeger came through, and I realized that he was much more than a folk singer. He told us about how the revolution was in his youth. He was a faith-keeper and a master of ceremonies.

And now I find that I am about the same age as Pete Seeger was when he came to that jam. And that's what I want to be for you. I want to be a faith keeper. I even got a letter from Pete this year where he praised our work and challenged me to be more of an activist. In my church, that is an instruction from on high.

I want to tell you that you have a long

and noble history and you never have to be ashamed of yourselves. You are the artists and the intellectuals and the compassionate faith-keepers of our culture.

The Farm midwives are also masters of the natural ceremony. When we were on the caravan we had some women with us who were going to deliver while we were still on the road. At the time of the first delivery, no one had as yet stepped up to the plate and said that they were a midwife.

We were at Northwestern University and just before the time for me to go and address the students, one of the pregnant women said she was going into labor. She asked me to deliver the baby, possibly on the grounds that I was a Marine veteran and had had a few courses in emergency medicine. Ina May and some of the other women said that I already had a date to talk to all these people and they would cover it. That was fine with me. I wasn't sure how battlefield wound dressings related to childbirth anyway.

The birth went beautifully, and I was able to come back to the auditorium after the break and announce that a healthy baby boy had been born in a bus in the parking lot. The crowd cheered.

For Ina May, the experience was profound. She saw the mother become beautiful and radiant and realized that there were heavy psychic powers associated with childbirth. Her attention had been attracted.

The next birth we had was in Ann Arbor. When we got back to San Francisco, we liked the north-central US and Nashville, Tennessee, as having nice sane people who related to us as young people instead of some bunch of brain-damaged anti-patriots. We ended up going to Nashville because it was warmer—the weather, not the people.

Ina May and some of the other women were going to try to be prepared for this birth and not be taken unawares. They had found a midwife manual and studied up some. One of the women was in that hippy superstitious place where she thought that studying the part about starting a baby who didn't start on its own might manifest it and make it happen. The chapter on resuscitation was not studied. (That lady got over all of that stuff too and later became an MD and oncologist herself.)

I was in my bus waiting when one of the women came running breathlessly to tell me that the baby had come. She said to me, "Oh, it's so beautiful." But her face told me there was something wrong, with such a strong, tragic impression that I jumped out the door and ran to the birthing bus as fast as I could go. Sure enough, the women were sitting around the bed, not knowing what to do about the small, still, gray baby. I saw she needed a breath. The Marine training had at least taught me how to do mouth-to-mouth resuscitation.

I picked up the baby and said, "In cases like this, give the baby a breath," and gently gave a small baby-sized breath. Her mouth was kind of sticky and was stuck shut. As soon as I gave her the breath and opened her up, she sucked in a good lungful, and you could see the pink color flow through her as the oxygen suffused her blood. She started up nicely and the mother and midwives were delighted.

The mother sends me a card for the baby's birthday each year and tells me what good grades she makes. I felt like we were home free about oxygen deprivation when the mother told me her daughter was in the 99th percentile on her national English tests.

This was the occasion where Ina May had her calling to be a midwife and to be sure that all women and babies had their best chance for life and health. As for me, I'm not even considered backup anymore. The midwives are so well-trained and developed by now that they have statistics for 2,000 births that are better than hospitals all over the country.

In their work, the midwives have done many important things, but one of my favorites is proving the hippy energy assumptions in the objective arena of childbirth.

The midwives prove that vibes are real and that they make a difference. Their excellent statistics are the result, in large part, of their understanding of birth as a psychic event as well as a material event. The medical establishment has taken the mechanical part about as far as it can be sanely taken and maybe a little past that. The midwives have better numbers than the doctors from recognizing the spiritual dimension of childbirth.

The hospital closest to us in Tennessee has a 44% Cesarean-section rate. A Cesarean-section means taking the baby out surgically through the belly, from a belief that the mother can't do it the normal way. Our midwives' Cesarean-section rate is 1.7%.

Ina May is an original founder of the Tennessee Midwives' Association and the Midwives' Alliance of North America. Midwifery has gone from brown rice to gourmet. Ina May and our other midwives are invited to speak at international conventions and lecture to doctors at grand rounds in hospitals. Their statistics and techniques are written up in medical journals. They are masters of the ceremonies of a very high art and science.

My poetry teacher at San Francisco State College, Mark Linenthal, said: "If you don't know if there is a God or not, then that is the next thing you have to find out." He had me videotaped for the San Francisco State College Poetry Archive. I said, "But Mark, I'm not a poet." He said, "Nonsense, of course you are." He also said: "I never hold grass. I never own grass. I never buy grass. But if someone hands me a joint, I take a hit." He was a Ph.D. with tenure. Those were his personal limits on safety.

Part of being a grownup is controlling your relationship with the whole material plane, not just dope. If you find yourself bummed out by not having any pot or putting your bad mood and bad temper on your friends about it, you should quit for a while until you are less attached. If you find yourself doing something dishonest to get the money to score cannabis, you're in trouble.

In the early days I smoked fairly low-grade weed, the cheapest I could get, but I quickly found it was like buying a small motorcycle: you always want the next size faster. There did come a time in the late Sixties when I was in the flow of so many hippies that I had immense amounts of cannabis passing through all the time. I had a kilo of Acapulco Gold in my sock drawer and I'd fill up my pouch every morning. I'd smoke that whole pouch in the course of the day. And I realized that I'd run myself up to a place where I was pretty jaded. I was getting pretty high off the first one I smoked, and the rest were not really doing that much to me. Then I saw that I would stay higher and higher for longer if I would smoke less and pace myself out. I realized I had been abusing it. You can get higher on one number of Gold a day than you can on too many.

Becoming jaded on grass is disrespectful to the grass. I think we devalue grass a bit sometimes by toking up and running out to do something else instead of sitting back and waiting for it to come on. When you turn on, you ought to relax and let it happen. Some people turn on for years and are always distracted by music or television or a party. They never get into the upper reaches of cannabis. That's the place where you have to be a little deliberate and ceremonial.

You can be stoned and then have to open the door to someone you don't know, and pull yourself around and cope and then act like you're not stoned, and it brings you down. You have to act like you're stoned again to get back to where you were. You have to put yourself in the position that it's okay to be stoned. My business is taken care of, there's not a pot of beans that's going to burn, the kids are covered and not needing care, preferably you're out of the flow of telephones. Then you can take that deliberate space and time to sit back and let the grass do what it wants to do (pardon the anthropomorphism), which is open you up and leave you compassionate. It is also perfectly fine to get stoned and have fun, which is another kind of prayer.

For regular daytime use, I seldom turn on before late in the afternoon. If I'm busy and I got stuff to do, I turn on when I settle down to watch the evening news. And then I might smoke another one around the middle of the evening before bedtime. At most, I might be sharing three a day. I get a lot of mileage from that, and I don't get too jaded. I like to do one late in the evening because I like to sleep on a leftover stone, it's such a nice comfortable sleep.

All that newspaper talk about grass and gangs is untrue. There was even a book, written by a member of a "stomping" gang in the very tough Bedford-Stuyvesant section of New York City. He said that they fought on alcohol and speed and used grass to come back down to a peaceful mode after the fight.

While the War on Drugs may have had no positive effect on coke or violence, it has run the price of grass sky-high and the quality and supply way down. It is so wearing to hear even the President pass on that tired old myth of the ten-times-stronger pot (than the kind he smoked) as a rationale for prohibition. I see some of the best pot in the world. Where the hell is this legendary 10x pot? How come teenagers have to be protected from it and I can't even find any? No one I know has quit smoking, however. They just smoke smaller joints and less frequently. Now the question is, "Are your streets any safer?" I think not. Any violence associated with pot has to do with the nature of money, not the nature of pot.

Here's a story about our neighbors that's illuminating about the nature of pot: In our neighborhood, drunk driving is a main cause of death among young men, followed by gunshot wounds. There is a family who had a younger boy who was a drinker and a hard driver and was always wrecking cars and getting in fights and hurting himself or other people. As time went on, he got into reefer and drifted away from alcohol and he cooled out. His family, a bunch of old Tennessee farmers, saw that change in him. They had a family meeting and gathered the oldest members of the family down to the youngest members. The family patriarch said, "We know that you have been smoking that marijuana. Here's the way we feel about it. It looks like you're going to get to live to be a man and not get killed right away. Now, if this reefer is what you do, and it helps you that way, we will just do it with you." That whole family changed over from beer and moonshine to marijuana, and you never hear a word about them anymore.

It really saddens me to see guns involved in the grass trade. It's really bad whenever I see it. Marijuana should certainly be decriminalized, and probably coke and heroin as well. Decriminalizing marijuana would have the effect of bringing 25 million pot smokers in from the cold and allow them to become worthy citizens. (Or to be treated as worthy citizens, as the vast majority of them already are.) Everyone in jail for simple pot possession, who was not involved with guns or hard drugs, should have amnesty. It is the least the government can offer. They actually deserve financial compensation for the imposition.

On the other end of the spectrum, taking the profit out of cocaine would confound the coke lords more than anything else you could do.

When grass is identified with wealth instead of consciousness, it isn't good. Grass isn't like that.

Grass is benign and reassuring. Acid was like trying to balance on the nose of an orca whale as it comes out of the water. If you leaned a little too far into the windstream, it would catch you and carry you away. Acid has a little death flavor. Grass doesn't. Grass is wholesome. With Acid there's always a little bit of trepidation. "Am I going to make it with an okay stomach? Or is it going to wreck me? Am I going to bum?"

Grass gives you a good appetite and makes you hungry and enjoy food. Grass is an ally. It naturally engenders spirituality in the people that do it. Grass is not sexually based. Boys and girls like it equally well. Grass will actually help allay fear and paranoia and bad vibes. It has a beneficial effect.

Sometimes people do get paranoid on grass, but it is almost always something that can be fixed by talking about it with good friends. It is not intrinsic to the grass.

Most of the time, if I'm called to sort out a big family fight, I come in, sit down and start rolling joints until everybody says, "That's enough." Then each person gets to tell their story, without interruptions, until they feel that they have said all that they need to. Mostly that fixes it, since as the truth emerges and can be seen by everyone involved, the answers become apparent too.

One of the things about grass that is neat is that if you get a little meditative, it gives you a sense of perspective on yourself. You see yourself as one person among a whole world population rather than as an absolute personal ego. This tends to make it easier for your friends to stand you.

6 GOOD LOVING

Your immune system can be damaged, according to published medical reports, by psychic events like feeling betrayed or having an anger fit or being the recipient of an anger fit. There are also psychic factors that can enhance your immune system, like good loving. It's the people's healing machinery. You can be on the edge of catching a cold and move that energy around and rev up your sexual furnace and burn that cold out and heal yourself. That's one of the most important uses of grass. It crosses the line between medical and spiritual; it's good for your health and it's good for your soul.

People who are kept from having a powerful vibratory sex life are more likely to go crazy and have hard times, and get crossways with family and friends. Our dominant religious culture doesn't want you to have a powerful sex life. This culture tries to shut it down every time it sees it. People would have higher-class sexual fantasies if they were permitted.

What I mean by permitted is that there is a maximum of stimulation and exploitation by the advertising and entertainment and clothing industries of the sexual reflex as it exists in humankind. The people don't get to build their own archetypes; they are force-fed them by the mass communications industry.

The media are not concerned with taste or decency except as something imposed from the outside. They haven't a clue about clean healing magic. What they want are images that cannot be ignored, to help sell their products. At the same time, part of the culture attempts to impose puritanical sexual codes on the rest of the culture by capturing school boards and trying to amend the Constitution.

I believe that people, if not jacked around by the advertising industry on the one hand and the religious right on the other, would derive beautiful and loving sexual representations that would be part of the traditional teaching information of the culture. Our culture is weird. It is okay to use breasts to sell car parts but not okay

for a mother to nurse a baby where someone might see. This is perverse in the technical sense of the term. It is indicative of the
decadence of our culture that the fine art of
the centuries is considered dirty by the
American religious right. For them, sex has
only two results, babies or sin.

I've seen couples that were having a hard
time sexually try cannabis and have it just
open their vibes until they were able to re-
establish the thing that made them want to
be together in the first place. They repaired
their relationship with the increased communication grass brings. I've seen a fair
amount of that.

But I also notice—and this is one of the
real places where grass and sex come together—sometimes making love in the morning
causes the grass I smoked the previous
evening to come on again. It wakes that grass
up and I get restoned making love the morning after. It just shows how the vibes are so
human and the grass is so natural.

Whenever grass comes through, it has different weights, different flavors and different effects. Whenever my wife and I run
into any good loving weed, we just set that

aside and don't use it for anything else. It's so good, it's a shame to waste it watching a movie. It's always so miraculous, to have *aura* be not just a word, but a thing you can touch and feel with the same senses you feel sunlight and warmth.

People going into their old age who are loving couples should be nicely sexually active just as long as they live, barring disease. My father, I was told, was sexually active until he was 89. And only a prostate operation kept him from continuing onward. He said he thought it should last your whole life. My great-grandfather conceived his last son when he was 75. I know it's not like you get over the hill at 40 and it's no fun anymore. I mean, I am 61 and I love it.

I knew an old couple in Canada in the late Seventies who had a good sex life. She was 68 and her boyfriend was 75. They told me about their meditation room upstairs, which was their loving room. There were psychedelic tie-dyes and batiks on the walls and beautiful posters and artwork. It was a real tripping room. Part of their ceremony was to smoke grass. They would get out their stash and go through the ritual, separating the seeds, doing it all nice and tidy, and turn on together preparatory to making love. They had excellent times and really cared for and enjoyed each other. They flirted with each other like teenagers. It's nice to see someone have such a good sex life at such an age.

While I was visiting them (Ina May and I were there on midwife business), there was another visitor. He was about 35, and when he was introduced he said that he was a sex therapist. It hit me a little wrong for this young whippersnapper to claim to be a sex therapist in front of these old, advanced Tantric Yogis and I said, sort of dead, "Yeah, me too." And the old man laughed a big horse laugh and said, "Yes, yes, very good, me too." They must be in their nineties by now, and I hope they are still getting it on.

Flirting is one of the telepathic languages. The most subtle signals and communications are brought to bear to build a strong nonverbal base from which telepathy can arise.

The human mind is such a heavy computer and classy de-encryption device: All input is played forward and backwards, scanned for puns in all familiar languages, tested for truth and sexual references and context-referenced as a constantly running set of subroutines that you don't have to pay any conscious attention to.

Flirting is basically a cumulative exchange of signals, signs and vibes, both conscious and unconscious, that usually culminates in agreements that can range from agreeing to be friends and flirt a little for sport when we meet, to agreeing to get married, be together forever and have children. Some of the best and most skillful flirting is that which goes on between folks who have known each other a long time and can tell the slightest clues and make a sweet and bawdy agreement nonverbally, and pretty quickly too. People have a sexy aura. A lot of folks have it without any augmentation at all, too. Real flirting isn't hunter and hunted, but an unspoken cooperation to bring the event to the desired conclusion for both parties.

I love to flirt and I "speak" many dialects of flirtation. It wasn't always that way, though. I didn't learn to speak boy/girl flirtation until I was a grownup. Of course, by then it was too late. Now I understand that boy/girl flirting is just one of the many languages and dialects involved.

One of the neatest ones I have learned is flirting with older women. They are very good! Years of practice has made them subtle and humorous. Flirting with babies is a whole other thing. Babies can flirt long before they can talk. One of my favorite sports is flirting with babies at long distance in the supermarket. Of course one has to be careful not to go overboard and get in trouble with their mothers. Flirting with geezers has its own rewards. I love to get a smile out of some sour-looking old coot. Most of these kinds of flirtation are not the negotiation kind, but are engaged in for their own sake.

It was hippy ladies that showed me the joy of unattached flirting on grass for the pure sport of it, almost as an art form.

My father showed me how to walk through auto garages or farm-implement stores and say, "Hey!" with just the right, polite but disinterested tone that neither fawns nor dismisses but merely acknowledges.

One of the things that I love most about grass is the way it enhances all these different kinds of communication.

At a Sunday morning service in Golden Gate Park, where it was customary to smoke cannabis at sunrise, I noticed a lady friend standing about 15 feet away from where I was, and we smiled and nodded "Good morning" to each other. We were good friends, and she blew me a kiss and gave a humorous sexy wiggle. When she did that I felt it touch me in my vibes as clear as day, and we both looked back at each other questioningly, like, "Did you feel that?" And the very fact that we had looked that question at each other showed that we had both felt that clear, sweet, sexy vibe. She looked at me mischievously and gave a small and subtle but potent bump-and-grind which flashed a lovely warm rush in my body. I wondered if I could do it too and *reached* to see if I could connect from my end to her. She closed her eyes and shuddered delicately. It was as if we were two violin strings and the bow would stroke us both at the same time, or that one was stroked and the other resonated. Soon we were both smiling broadly in appreciation of the strength and delicious sexy warmth we were feeling together.

Now some might think that was a funny way to be carrying on Sunday morning, but in a church that respects the telepathic medium between us all as the real and true holy spirit, it was perfectly apropos. We were not only having a very loving and intimate moment while standing 15 feet apart; but we were a living *mudra* of soul communication to any who had eyes to see.

We just made up a little ball of that juice and threw it back and forth like playing catch with a tennis ball. We were both in agreement that it was okay to do that, and we both could feel the juice, and we both knew it could be directed and returned as well as received.

In the Sixties, like many of us who studied Vedanta, I was into Tantric Yoga, and specifically *karezza*, which puts a big value on not ejaculating. I have come to feel that the orgasm is such an electromagnetic, telepathic mind-cleaner and reset button that it shouldn't be avoided. If you're wise enough not to carry your troubles over past them, they can give you a new start.

One of the things that grass helped teach me that made a big difference in my life was a view of sex that was not primarily procreational. By this, I mean not only the view that sex is for reproduction only and any other use is sin, but even the idea that sex cannot be extricated from reproduction.

Thinking procreationally makes you look at the opposite sex as breeding stock. This is what makes people marry absolutely unsuitable mates who are pretty and healthy to look at. Sometimes short women choose tall men, or vice versa, in an unconscious wish to make a taller next generation. In ancient England, tall and large women were prized for the potential of producing big strong children, because war was a hand-to-hand business and size counted.

Not thinking procreationally makes you less competitive and less jealous. Jealousy is real primal stuff and it has to do with reproduction. People are just as ruthless as lions when it comes to what they want to do with their genes. It takes intelligence and hard work to fit these instincts into the discourse of a civilized world.

Some researchers say that it is to men's genetic advantage to scatter their seed far and wide. The same researchers say that it is to women's genetic advantage to have the same father for all their children, to reinforce his tendency to protect the family and nurture the children. This is thinking procreationally. What we need to be able to do is make a distinction between vibration and reproduction.

Grass was a great, if unknown and unappreciated, ally in the women's movement because it made so many guys less procreationally driven and more vibrationally driven sexually, and made them easier to get along with and not so demanding.

It is a problem in this country where even the thousands of teenagers who have babies are not enough to move the fundamentalist Right to allow effective sex education in school. There is an old right-wing Southern legislator named Jeremiah Denton who understands better than that. He said, when he heard the scary teenage birth figures, "Hasn't anybody ever heard of heavy petting?"

If you are not thinking procreationally, there is no battle of the sexes. There is a co-operation. The object is not to impregnate or be impregnated, but to share a healing, loving ceremony that leaves both partners lighter, freer and more healthy.

I feel I'm trying to talk about Tantra without saying Tantra. The thing about Tantra that is relevant to our generation of seekers is that we came down the psychedelic path and were exposed to marijuana and peyote and magic mushrooms. These things greatly increase and augment the presence and ability to feel the kind of vibes that are felt in Tantra. There are a lot of people, who might not have had the real dedication and self-discipline to go ahead and discover that kind of stuff without any help, who were able to find it out with the help of cannabis. It was such a good thing for people to learn those skills, whether they kept on smoking dope or not. It became a permanent part of their lives to understand those ebbs and flows and feelings of spiritual loving.

You understand it not as a reproductive thing, but as a vibrational reality that is worthy in itself. It is part of our first line of defense against disease to be easy and relaxed. The word disease means *dis*-ease, you are not eased. Loving can ease you. It is one of the most precious things that is commonly available to ordinary people.

Cannabis can make a tremendous difference in a person's relationships and add a whole new spiritual factor to a marriage. It also helps for a man and woman to understand each other intellectually to get into a place where they are cooperating and moving good vibes like that.

A lot of the time the path of communication between male and female is the sharing and displaying of archetypes and clichés, and not actually being who they really are. Cannabis is very good at dissolving this kind of role-playing and allowing real communication. I'm sure both sexes would be really relieved if they knew what the other one was really like. It is natural to feel love with someone with whom you have shared energy.

It's not that grass is an aphrodisiac, in the sense that it makes you want to get laid, which is what most people think an aphrodisiac is, but it is an amplifier and facilitator of natural sexual vibrations. And if somebody lives an uptight life and has trouble getting relaxed enough to actually get into that vibration, grass can really help them out. It helps them learn how to do it better so they can do better if they don't have grass. And if you're already pretty skilled and have a good loving relationship, grass can push you into spiritual realms. It's really very strong.

I've read some of the old books that say you're supposed to stroke the yoni one hundred times. That just means you're supposed to relax and let stuff flow and take as long as it takes to get to where you're going. You should be non-judgmental and non-goal-oriented, non-performance-directed. Know that you're going into something that's of mutual benefit to both parties. It's good for you, it's good to you. You're going to cooperate together, and it's not a question of, "Oh, my God, I lost my erection." Like streetcars, there will be another one coming along pretty soon. And if everybody knows that, then that's not the part we're doing now, and it's cool.

For good sense, as well as Tantric peace of mind, you must have your birth control together. I recommend the method the Farm put together, because it doesn't involve any chemicals and it lets you be completely free. We made a book about it called *A Cooperative Method of Natural Birth Control,* by Margaret Nofziger. It's a combination of two or three classical methods. Charting your menstrual cycle is one of the methods that help predict when you're going to ovulate. Learning to check your cervical mucus can let you know when you just did ovulate. Of course, in these high-tech times, there are little pocket microscopes that a lady can lick the lens of and look through to see if it creates "ferns," which let you know where you are in the cycle. If you get two or three of these systems working together, you can pinpoint ovulation.

We found on the Farm that women who use the system frequently get so in tune with themselves that they know when they are going to ovulate and can feel it happen. There's a name for it in German, *mittelsmertz.* That means "little pain in the middle."

It makes it not be mysterious when it's cool to make love and when it's not. You can be free of chemicals and appliances. It's simple and natural and free, so that's why I recommend it. Of course it requires a committed relationship and a strong, loving, spiritual agreement. People who are interested in this method of birth control can write the Book Publishing Company, PO Box 99, Summertown, TN 38483, and ask for it. If you are not in a safe relationship, in these times of AIDS and casual sex, condoms are appropriate for people who date. It could save your life.

7 STAY STRAIGHT WITH KIDS

We have been on the Farm for 25 years now; the Farm has grandchildren. It is kind of interesting to compare the Farm to the greater society, where by all accounts the teenagers are in deep trouble. Over the long haul and more recently, we have not had a child-pregnancy problem. We actually consider 18 to be fairly young to be having babies on the Farm. A lot of girls wait until their twenties to marry and have kids. We believe that is because there has been complete frankness with our kids. Sex education has been a normal part of growing up. Most of our kids spent part of their youth watching birth videos. This was not from some plan, just the reality that our young couples were forming their families and birth videos were shown in most of the houses at one time or another. It would never occur to our kind of hippies to send anyone out of the room because something real was going to be shown.

We started a satellite-TV-receiver business and began to have satellite dishes for some of the houses. People said, "Aren't you afraid that your kids are going to tune into the skin flicks on the Playboy channel?"

We said, "Our kids would probably say, 'What is that lady's dilation? When is she going to crown? How long before the baby comes?'" We feel that our kids are very sane about sex and we are pleased and relieved. Our kids are pretty sane about grass, too. I often am amused by my position in the United States, where I am in the flower-child, reefer, spiritual Left. Among the hippies, I am moderate to conservative, especially about dope and children.

I don't think children should use cannabis. When children get an early introduction to cannabis, too often they go immediately to the limits of habituation and supply. It becomes something that structures their time, and they neglect their education. If I had known I was going to need to remember my Spanish verbs for the rest of my life, I would have studied harder at the time. It's a lot harder to learn them now. I feel really strongly about children getting a good education. And that doesn't mean they all have to be businessmen or machinists. They all have different talents and their education should be flexible enough so that they get to develop those talents.

Back in the Sixties, when we were freaking our brains out, a lot of people turned on kids who were too young. At the Farm, as we've evolved as a community, it has become evident that we'd rather our kids didn't start turning on early. We don't want to distract them from their essential kidness.

Keeping cannabis out of the hands of small children is one of the most important and difficult questions that hip parents as well as square parents face. You can't just depend on keeping it out of their hands, either. The best thing would be if you had never lied to them and you were friends and they would respect your wishes. A lot of our ethic came from young people and it is a mistake to think that they can't understand anything heavy.

When the hippies came along they had

this sweet young ethic, and they were fair and tried to be good scouts. They were so idealistic and wanted so much to be good, that I just could not help but love them. I took the ethic as it came from them and I cleaned it up and edited it and abstracted from it the things that were, if not new and original, at least beautiful to be seen in this time frame. I fed it back to them as a cleaned-up version of their own thing and they recognized it, they knew this was our ethic. It was magical because when I was saying the real stuff it was very stoned, everybody recognized it, and it made it an incredible fabric of consciousness.

In that same way, children can recognize when their parents are telling the truth or not, especially if their parents have always told them the truth in the past.

Many people are worried about children becoming attached to grass and having it take over their lives. I also think it is very important for children to achieve a work ethic before starting a relationship with grass. It seems to me that grass is a lovely icing on the cake of life but that it is not to be substituted for the cake.

Parents are concerned about the "amotivational syndrome" or the idea that grass-smokers tend not to work and to be lazy and not fulfill their obligations. Vera Rubin, who did the amotivational-syndrome study in Jamaica, found that people in Jamaica work hard while smoking tropical ganja of great strength. She showed that the syndrome doesn't always affect grownups. I think it is still a serious concern with children.

Kids don't need any extraneous things standing between them and learning their life tools. It's such a heavy emotional time for them, with their hormones coming in and all, that it's hard for them to be more amplified than they already are. Sometimes cannabis puts kids on ego trips. (Sometimes cannabis puts adults on ego trips.) I think it makes them think they are already grown up and they don't need to try.

Official Farm policy has been no turning on children under the age of 18. We told the kids, "If you're under 18, it's unfair to put a grownup between you and the law."

However, there's a ceremonial place when they are old enough, when a teenager takes up as much space as a grownup, eats as much food as a grownup and works as much as a grownup. They participate in creating the adult community vibe. It isn't fair at that point to treat them as children. I think some teenagers can be damaged by being excluded from important ceremonies. At the same time, I'm sure that some kids will continue to use cannabis as an outlaw thing. Some of them can even handle it, but many cannot.

The classic relationship with grass that the early hippies had was that it's better when shared with friends. You can't get really high with a bad attitude. Kindness and sweetness exhilarates your stone. Stolen grass doesn't get you as high. The old original hippie ethic really counts and that's the thing we need to transmit to the kids.

The only way kids can be spoken to about anything heavy is straight, person-to-person. If you talk down to them they will detect it down to one part in a million. You must tell the truth; they will know if you don't. It's more important to be honest with your kids than it is to smoke cannabis. Either tell them you do it, or don't do it. If this is the situation you find yourself in, you should consider making a major lifestyle change. If you have to lie to the kids, you are probably lying to the neighbors too. You might need to find a better neighborhood.

If you can come to a good peaceful agreement in the family, where the kids respect the adults' privacy and the adults don't insult the kids' intelligence, you might not have to move.

Our kids have always known right up front. We've never hidden a thing from them. We could usually tell easily if our kids tried it. We learned that was the time to get straight about it. It wasn't the biggest thing in the world. But we're in a little Shangri-La here, where we can have our own ways and it works.

If you're a parent living in the big city with a kid going to a public school, and they have a turn-your-parents-in program at that school, you have a problem. I hate to see these programs that get kids to turn in their parents. That is absolutely morally wrong and an intrusion into family life that even a Republican should hate.

Let your kids know where you're at all the way down the line. I know a hippy woman, an intelligent working mother who smokes grass herself, who was having a hard time keeping her teenage boy from smoking. He was the kind who would have bailed out on school, but his mother was determined that he stay in school and not smoke. She bought a commercial piss-test kit and tested her boy until he respected her wishes and gave up pot for school.

When I first heard about it, I have to admit that I was shocked. It was drastic, but I have to say that I respected her moves. She did not give up on him, she didn't write him off. She insisted on her point without involving the authorities. Her boy came out fine and loves and respects his mother. I am not recommending this as a practice. I am just saying that if you have a kid who is at serious risk and is in trouble, a parent's prerogatives go that far. It beats hell out of calling the cops or social workers down on them and risking losing custody.

By far, your best chance is honesty, because if you throw a surprise down on them, they might just turn you in to one of those snitch-your-parents-off programs. Even if they don't, it will confuse them. If you act like you didn't do it and you did, and you are dishonest with them, they will disrespect you. That's a far more dangerous thing than having to quit smoking. Staying straight with your kids is the most important thing.

8 THE POLITICS OF SPIRITUALITY

I guess it was the French historian Alexis de Tocqueville who said that the United States was the only country to go from barbarism to decadence without an intervening period of civilization. I think that as the century draws to a close, we are at a turning point of history. We are the generation that has the responsibility to redeem the American dream.

Redeem is a technical term. It means to make an estimation, as in "I deem it just." It means we have to take a new look at our society and see if it still stands for the same thing. We have to redeem it and then fix it. If ignorance and greed and racism continue to force the direction of the country, we could enter that decadence so deeply that we might not see real freedom return for a generation, if at all.

I have become more and more concerned the last few years, as I have seen my native country lose contact with reality and do real things that cause real damage to real people for the sake of mere words and erroneous ideas. We are in a position where the base of truth of our culture is so eroded that it is almost unrecognizable. It is difficult for young people to tell what kind of country and world we are supposed to be working for.

I blame it partly on the nature of the material plane and partly on the Republicans and the greed that they teach, most of it, but I also realize that it is not just them either. It is really a population explosion on a worldwide scale, far out of anyone's control. As the world gets more populated there are fewer ways to make a living, fewer economic niches. People start looking for other things to do, like taking care of each other, that used to be done for love or for duty, and start charging money for them.

It gets to where the kindness that is the grease in society that keeps us from squeaking is getting used up and society begins to squeak more loudly. People who would have been cared for by their children or relatives or extended family or even the next-door neighbor perhaps, have to shell out $35 an hour for someone to be their companion and hang out with them and maybe put a couple of loads in the washer for them. This is some of the decadence of our time.

It seems to me that when service and taking care of people have become something that we are going to barter and trade for, then to go out and give service out of the goodness of your heart gets to be a real in-your-face revolutionary act. I am going to continue to live as if there is such a thing as love and duty. We used to just talk about love, but if you are to speak about love now you have to say love and duty; just like we used to talk about "peace," but as grownups we learned that we have to talk about peace and justice.

We seem to be in a kind of political entropy or running down, like the Indian concept of the Kali Yuga, or decadent fourth quarter of creation. This is not just to say that everything is going to hell. Things are truly up for grabs as well. There are also great chances for advancement, but not without work.

What I mean by "base of truth" is that a country that was formed in one great cataclysm of revolution, like the United States, begins with a clear enough public self-concept that people actually geared up for a great social effort and made great personal sacrifices to change the paradigm.

As time goes on, the concept is tested by greed, self-interest and reality. Laws are changed and amended at the behest of lobbyists for special financial interests, sometimes to close loopholes and sometimes to open them, and the law becomes cluttered with legal fictions that become calcified into the code and are, legally, treated as truth.

If a lawmaker wants to put the screws to marijuana smokers, he can propose a law that puts marijuana in the same category with heroin. This is scientifically untrue but has been made legally true just about everywhere. These lies of convenience obscure truth and add to the cultural burden of untruth that weighs down our society. It obscures our national identity.

We forget who we are. This is wrong. We

must never forget that we are the people who thumbed our nose at royalty and have made it stick for over 200 years. That is what makes America important, not the gross national product.

What Martin Luther King meant by "live out the meaning of our creed" was that even though the United States was originally designed for the freedom of different kinds of white male Protestants, we know that in all decency, it should include women, people of color and all religions.

When the Democrats have the hammer, they pass laws and rules that at least claim to be for the sake of the common people, whether they end up that way or not. When the Republicans are in power they try to recover the ground for the rich people and the fight becomes more important than the well-being of the people, and the truth of the laws, which the people have to live by, is lost in the ideological wrangling.

We are asked to believe that having insurance companies suck billions of dollars out of the health-care system doesn't make it more expensive.

We are asked to believe that the videotape of Rodney King being beaten by the police is not clear evidence of police riot and racism.

We are told that nicotine is not addictive, that selling guns into the population doesn't escalate violence and that justice is not for sale, in spite of the clear evidence of millionaires walking away untouched from capital crimes.

We are told by doctors that we have "the best health-care system in the world," even though our medical system is one of the most unfair and most expensive in the Western world and leaves 44 million people uninsured.

We are told that poverty and other social circumstances have nothing to do with the crime rate and that it is just coincidental that one in four young black men goes to jail.

We are told that marijuana causes violence and that it is addictive, has no medical or economic uses and that it causes brain damage and impotence and makes men grow breasts.

We are told that the prohibition against cannabis is because of its extreme danger, even though it has been proven safer than aspirin and less addictive than coffee. President Nixon's own commission returned the verdict that cannabis could be the safest substance in the pharmacopoeia.

We are told that the extreme sanctions against cannabis, so Draconian as to effectively repeal the constitutional safeguards, are to protect the public and the country. The prosecutors are instructed to get the people who are under suspicion to make a plea bargain to save the expense of a jury trial.

Lawyers are officers of the court. To understand this one only has to notice that there is a fence in a courtroom between the people and the legal establishment. This fence is guarded by armed marshals. Your lawyer is free to cross that fence at will, but you are not. Even though you are paying your lawyer, his first allegiance is not to you but to the court. He is going to see that judge and those police officers and those state's attorneys tomorrow and the next day. They are who he sees socially. He is not going to see you after you are done with court, win or lose.

In effect, your lawyer assists the prosecutors to get you to cop a plea to save wear and tear on the court. You have to sign a written plea agreement that tells the specifics of your deal, and how badly you can be screwed if you break the deal. The agreement also says that there is no deal. If you make any waves, the deal is off. Then you go into court and swear before the judge that there is no deal and that you haven't been promised anything. If you don't swear to that, the deal is off. I want to say this again, in case you glossed over that last couple of paragraphs. *If you don't swear in open court that there is no deal, then the deal is off!*

The teeth in the system is that if there is no deal, you fall back on the federal guidelines, which give life in prison with no parole for a ton of pot. (I should say metric ton, 1,000 kilos.) For 50 to 100 kilos, the federal guidelines give five to 20 years with no parole. The only way out is the deal, which you have to swear hasn't been offered to you. The deal is actually unconstitutional, and you have to tell the judge that you understand that and it is okay with you to not have the usual constitutional protections.

This is to protect the judge and the court from any legal repercussions for playing fast and loose with your rights. The entire weight and thrust of all this legal chicanery is to give the prosecutors tools to force you to turn in your friends. It is intimidation by bludgeon. The reason that they think all this is okay is because marijuana is so evil and by extension *you* are so evil that it doesn't matter what is done to you. This is exactly the kind of crap that the Constitution was designed to protect us from. This is also why the religious Right has no real respect for the Constitution.

The edifice of legal fictions—lies—has grown so large and the pillar of truth that it stands on has been so eaten away that a collapse is likely. We have come nearly 180° from our original revolutionary first cause. The United States has the most people in prison of any country in the "free" world. Building prisons is one of the biggest growth industries. Five hundred thousand people are arrested annually for marijuana. People have 20, 30, 50 years of prison time for having or selling cannabis.

This brings me to the reason for doing this book with HIGH TIMES. The cultural wars have been declared on us by Newt Gingrich and the far Right. They say that the troubles of the United States started in the 1960s and the problems were all caused by the hippies.

This is another of the big untruths. The Sixties were one of this country's finest hours. Many changes that have been wrought in this country were done by people like us. In great measure, it was hippies and beatniks who helped go into the South and tell them that the outright segregation they had going on was not cool. A lot of hippy people were in on that. We helped get us out of Vietnam. We helped topple Richard Nixon. We helped educate about nukes. We helped pioneer attention to the environment and endangered species. We aided and supported native peoples, both in the United States and overseas. I am proud of our hippy heritage.

It is with this information and this background that I come to a conclusion that gives me no satisfaction.

When the crime is so minor, having marijuana, and the punishment is so unreasonable, taking people's homes and years of their lives, as well as a very real Twentieth-century shunning, one is forced to look for deeper motives. I have come to believe that it is not the proscription of a substance but the systematic oppression of a certain kind of people. There have been a whole series of decisions made, on local, state and federal levels, to the effect that hippies, by which is meant any committed liberal persons, are undesirable and are to be banned, interdicted, harassed, discouraged, arrested and pee-tested. It is a blatant use of police power to frighten and intimidate millions of people into giving up a heartfelt spiritual practice and lifestyle.

There are probably 25 million marijuana smokers in the United States alone, as well as millions more who if not smokers now are still sentimental about it. The oppression to which I refer is for the purpose of keeping these millions of people off balance to minimize their political power. All those 500,000 pot smokers doing time are out of the political process, present but not able to vote. The urine test is the loyalty oath of the Nineties. The hippies are this season's Jews, this season's Reds, and Newt is this season's Joe McCarthy.

I cannot understand why war is made on these people when marijuana is not the problem. Cocaine and heroin are causes of great social damage. No one robs liquor stores or turns tricks to buy pot. That is done to buy narcotics or speed. People don't do desperate things for pot because it isn't addictive. Sometimes I think it's just safer for the law to pick on hippies than heavily armed Mafia or cartel drug lords.

Who are all these people? We are the yeast that makes the dough rise. And it's not just us, there's been people like us for centuries. Before there were hippies, there were beatniks, before there were beatniks there were bohemians. The European counterculture ran away from Nazi Germany. They brought hundreds of thousands of artists and musicians and writers into this country. Before that there were people like George Bernard Shaw and Voltaire and all the way back to Socrates. There have always been that fraction of people who have said,

"I want to see the truth." We were never intended to be a take-over-the-world culture, but we are a cultural vitamin without which any society is not healthy.

This is not just my opinion. Look what happened when big-city television came to Tennessee. Back in May 1993 we got a call from the *Columbia Herald*, located in one of our closest towns, a town in which we have done a lot of business. They have followed us from our arrival, to being busted, to me and my three friends doing time, to us doing overseas relief and development work in Guatemala and Lesotho. They had called to warn me the new NBC show Jane Pauley got for leaving *The Today Show* was doing a story on the Farm. The caller said, "Tell Stephen to look out, NBC was asking about marijuana." The people at the newspaper were concerned NBC might not be good to us. A day or two later they called back with another message:

"We have decided to do a story about the Farm to show NBC how to treat you."

When the story came out, we were blown away. It was a two-page spread with the words "The Farm...The Farm...The

Farm…" in a 72-point headline across the top of both pages. There were six feature stories and six photos, all done in such a lovely, friendly and positive fashion that we got permission to have it reprinted as a double-sided tabloid-size flyer. We use it for a "Farm Report" to hand out to visitors and people who inquire by mail. We think that this is "bread on the water" that came back to us from being decent to the Tennesseans.

It was so sweet our neighbors cared for us and wanted to protect us, that we didn't mind at all about Jane Pauley's show being canceled. We thought it was very cool that our neighbors love us back.

When I was invited to be a celebrity judge at the 1995 Cannabis Cup, I experienced a moment of disbelief at my excellent good fortune. I thought, "You mean we get to go to Holland and smoke a lot of different kinds of dope and decide which is best and give each other prizes? Far out! This sounds like something some hippies thought up!"

In the ensuing few weeks, whenever I told someone that I was to be a guest judge in the marijuana championships, I saw that same moment of disbelief in their eyes. Then, in most cases, the next question was, "But how do you clear your palate? How can you tell if this is the last one coming on slow or the next one coming on fast?"

That would prove to be one of the main questions in the following days.

Steve Hager, the editor of HIGH TIMES, had invited us to be in New York a couple of days early for rehearsals with the band, dancers, clowns, jugglers, set designers, costume creators, roadies and general support crew. That good beginning was to set the keynote for the trip.

I loved traveling with the Cannabis Cup house band. When we moved to the Farm, one of the first things we did was to build a stage so we could congregate backstage and smoke with the band. This is, I think, one of the basic hippy dreams.

It was an education watching Garrick Beck work at sheep-dogging that bunch of anarchists into an elaborate stage presentation, armed with only a rough script and the craft he learned at his daddy's knee. He also had the help of a bunch of serious hippies who were also professional artists. The band kicked ass sweetly and soulfully. The jugglers were coordinated, the dancers pliable, beautiful and strong, the clowns funny, wise, magical and faintly troubling, as good clowns should be.

At first, Garrick had to round up their attention every few minutes, but as the crew understood the huge task that was ahead they moved into that sweet, reefer-propelled cooperation that makes rock-'n'roll enough fun to do even when there isn't money in it.

We went through bonding during the rehearsals, the plane trip and the ceremonies in Amsterdam that created friendships that are very likely to be lifelong.

We were on a mission. The ceremonies were at once high church and high camp. We loved each other for having the taste and courage to pull off such an incredible hoot. We also loved the Dutch for being so matter-of-fact about being so reasonable and intelligent. There was a little heartbreak in going home to my native country and knowing it to be a little less free than Holland.

I am not content to live in a country that

has become less free the longer that I have lived in it. That is the wrong direction and I pledge to work to try and fix it.

Some of the kinds of things that are in my mind are seeing that we are not going to actually win this revolution, not being a take-over-the-world movement. But even though we are not going to win it, we dare not lose it. We must continue to struggle, and probably it will be like it has for the last several thousand years, where the good people put out their best energy and try as hard as they can, and use every way that is decent to try to fight the trends of inhumanity, and we just about break even. As the Buddhists say, "That's life."

These grass-smokers are some of the nicest people in the world. They have a right to be heard and a right to life, liberty and the pursuit of happiness. They are kind people and try to be sensitive to others. Although cannabis is said to be a cause of violence, these people are so peaceful that they are ridiculed for it. They want to save the whales, they want to save the redwoods, they want to save the Indians, they want to save the ozone layer. They are basically trying to be good. They are my people and I love them. I hope this book gives them some heart and aid and courage and comfort and direction.

9
13 GUIDELINES FOR SANITY AND SURVIVAL

1

To understand the nature of delusion is very powerful; To know that one's own mind can put up an illusion that can fool the mind that made it is liberating. I once believed the *I Ching* had been written all those hundreds of years ago just to fool me in the here and now. The next thought I had was that I must be very paranoid to believe such a foolish thing. It was good to realize that I was paranoid. It was much better than thinking that the universe was somehow against me personally.

2

Up/Down handle: The way you are controls whether you are pushing up or down. The secret is to always pull up. Never pull down, not when in grief, not when in anger, not for revenge, not to demonstrate. Sometimes the up handle may seem to hurt at first, but it is always worth it. *Vale la pena*.

3

I am human and nothing human is alien to me. This was said by Terence, one of the old Roman playwrights. It just means that we all have the seeds of all human emotions and actions in us. What we actually do in this world is the result of our heredity, our environment and our free will. Under different circumstances, any of us might not have been as nice.

4

To love truth: To love truth is to recognize that truth is more important than what one may want to be true or what one may be afraid is true. The love of truth gives us something objective to strive for. When one understands the relationship between truth and sanity, it becomes natural to love truth.

5

It's not that you can't blow it, it's that you can always get it back. As long as you live and have free will, you can always change your act and get better.

6

Always tell yourself the truth in plain unvarnished terms about what you think of yourself, and what you do. You may not enjoy the knowledge and it might not make you like yourself, but it really helps to keep you from going crazy. Truth is the first defense against insanity.

7

Avoid the dichotomy as you would a deadly snake. Dichotomy is the idea that all conflicts and problems break into only two pieces that must be in opposition. Almost nothing in the real world is all light or all dark, or all good or all evil. To set the opposite extremes against each other in your thinking is to lose the subtlety and variety of the real world. It severely limits the possibilities of resolution of problems and conflicts.

8

You must have a personal code. There must be moral imperatives in your life. There must be things that you don't stoop to do and things that you are obliged to do. Having a personal code is like having a set of instruments to fly by in the dark or in a storm like an airplane. When an airplane is flying by instruments, there are dials and gauges on the instrument panel that tell the pilot if the plane is tilted to one side or the other and if altitude is being gained or lost and which way the plane is going. If it is dark or cloudy, the pilot has to fly by the information in the plane. In one's personal life, principles are the instruments that can be used to steer by when it is crazy out.

9

Know the difference between subjective and objective modes of thought. When you are subjective, you think only of the subject, that is, yourself. When you are objective, you can try to see the whole picture, not just those parts that affect your personal comfort. Truth is always objective.

10

Compassion is one of the antidotes for alienation. (In the 1800s, insanity was called alienation and what we call a headshrinker or psychiatrist was called an alienist.) Caring for other people helps take you outside yourself. Loving other people lets you know why it is important for you to do your best.

11

Principles are the rules that one lives by. Breaking your principles too often can help get you crazy. This is because your principles are the foundation of your identity. They help define who you are. Part of being sane is knowing who you are. This is what is meant by integrity.

12

When one understands the unsulliable nature of the intellect, it is no longer necessary to seek absolution for past sins. This is from the Tibetan tradition, as reported by W. Y. Evans-Wentz in *Tibetan Yoga and Secret Doctrines*.

I learned to understand this more fully when I was smoking some local grass that had come from a friend. I was surprised to find that it was very smart grass. Sometimes grass is sexy, sometimes it is sleepy, sometimes it is alert, sometimes it is artistic and sometimes it is smart. This grass was smart.

I began to think about the unsulliable nature of the intellect and I thought, this is like the difference between hardware crazy and software crazy. If you are hardware crazy, you need to learn to work around it or seek medical help. If you are software crazy, the unsulliable nature of the intellect comes into play.

A computer has two kinds of memory. One kind is called ROM, or *Read-Only*

Memory. This means that it is a permanent, unchangeable set of instructions
that tells the computer how to do normal
operations like work the mouse or make
type on the screen.

The other kind is called RAM, which
stands for *Random-Access Memory.* This
is the actual working memory of the computer. It can take any form, such as a game
or a check register or a word processor,
that the software dictates.

New computer users are told that there
is nothing you can say to a computer by
the keyboard that will break it or ruin it. If
you manage to confuse it enough with
conflicting instructions, the most that can
happen is it might lock up. In that case,
you just restart it and all those mistakes
are erased and the RAM comes back clean
and perfect. This is the unsulliable nature
of the random-access memory.

You can't break or ruin your mind by
anything you think. Your mind must be able
to think anything. It must be able to consider all alternatives, no matter how awful
or horrible. Your intellect is a perfect computer. If your mind couldn't consider all the

alternatives, that would be something wrong in itself. It does not make you crazy to think a crazy thought. You can look at that crazy thought and say to yourself, "My, what a crazy thought," and go on about your life without having any fear that your mind has been damaged or dirtied in any lasting way by that passing nutty thought. This is the unsulliable nature of the intellect.

13

I take great refuge in the benign indifference of the universe. That we are here at all is enough of a gift from the universe. That it is not against us either is excellent. As e.e. cummings said:

> *the gently falling snow*
> *doesn't give a soft white damn*